N E W L Y
N O T
E T E R N A L

GEORGE DAVID CLARK

NEWLY
NOT
ETERNAL

LOUISIANA STATE UNIVERSITY PRESS
BATON ROUGE

Published by Louisiana State University Press
lsupress.org

LSU PRESS PAPERBACK ORIGINAL

DESIGNER: Mandy McDonald Scallan
TYPEFACE: Whitman

COVER ILLUSTRATION: Elihu Vedder, *The Fates Gathering in the Stars,* 1887. The Art Institute of Chicago, Friends of American Art Collection.

LIBRARY OF CONGRESS CATALOGING-IN-PUBLICATION DATA

Names: Clark, George David, author.
Title: Newly not eternal / George David Clark.
Description: Baton Rouge : Louisiana State University Press, [2024]
Identifiers: LCCN 2023024675 | ISBN 978-0-8071-8127-0 (paperback) |
    ISBN 978-0-8071-8161-4 (epub) | ISBN 978-0-8071-8162-1 (pdf)
Subjects: LCGFT: Poetry.
Classification: LCC PS3603.L3634 N49 2024 | DDC 811/.6—dc23/
    eng/20230523
LC record available at https://lccn.loc.gov/2023024675

I have seen the burden God has laid on the human race.

He has made everything beautiful in its time.

—ECCLESIASTES 3:10–11

CONTENTS

ACKNOWLEDGMENTS

Grateful acknowledgment is made to the editors of the publications in which these poems previously appeared, sometimes in earlier versions and under different titles:

Antioch Review: "Little Black Bouquet: Muse"; *Arkansas International:* "Black Igloo"; *Bat City Review:* "Song of the Guardian Angel"; *Beloit Poetry Journal:* "Noon"; *Birmingham Poetry Review:* "Poltergeists"; *Cincinnati Review:* "Little Black Bouquet: Dim Time"; *Cortland Review:* "Kaleidoscope"; *Cumberland River Review:* "Gardensong"; *Ecotone:* "Hot Minute," "Postcard from Home," and "Washing Your Feet"; *Gettysburg Review:* "The Statue Gardens"; *Greensboro Review:* "Eyelash"; *Hampden-Sydney Poetry Review:* "Afterhere"; *Hopkins Review:* "Ultrasound"; *I-70 Review:* "Ambitious Circumcision"; *Literary Matters:* "A Few Keys," "The Latch," "Migraine," "Shiversong," and "Song of the Genie"; *The Moth:* "Mosquito"; *Ninth Letter:* "Song of the Imaginary Friend"; *Northwest Review:* "Midnight"; *Raintown Review:* "God Jokes"; *Rattle:* "Sun on Your Shoulders"; *Ruminate:* "Original Sins" and "Little Black Bouquet: Iscariot's Psalm"; *Salamander:* "Small God"; *Southern Poetry Review:* "Elsewhen" and "Yestermorrow"; *Southern Review:* "Loud Outs" and "Virga"; *Subtropics:* "Black Light" and "The First Supper"; and *Thrush Poetry Journal:* "Still Life."

"The Latch" and "Song of the Genie" were among a group of poems that received the 2019 Meringoff Poetry Award from the Association of Literary Scholars, Critics, and Writers (ALSCW).

"Loud Outs" and "Ultrasound: Your Picture" appeared on the Academy of American Poets' *poets.org.*

"Ultrasound: Your Picture" was also reprinted in *New Poetry from the Midwest 2019* (New American Press, 2021) and featured on WPSU's *Poetry Moment.*

"Washing Your Feet" and "Poltergeists" appeared on *Verse Daily*. "Washing Your Feet" was also reprinted in *Mid/South Sonnets* (Belle Point Press, 2023).

"Postcard from Home" was published as a letterpress broadside designed by Laurie Corral for the Bradford-Niedermann Broadside Series.

"Little Black Bouquet: Dim Time" had a second life as a letterpress broadside designed by Mary Heebner for the Kalamazoo Book Arts Broadside Series.

"Shiversong" and "Still Life" were reprinted in *Ecoflourishing and Virtue: Christian Perspectives Across the Disciplines* (Routledge, 2023).

"Yestermorrow" was reprinted in *Gracious: Poems from the 21st Century South* (Texas Tech University Press, 2020).

"Song of the Imaginary Friend" appeared on *E-Verse Radio*.

Thanks to the many friends and editors who challenged and encouraged early drafts of these poems and to those who most challenged and encouraged me as I wrote them: Dan Albergotti, Lisa Ampleman, James Arthur, Anna Lena Phillips Bell, Malachi Black, Brian Brodeur, David Eye, Jessica Faust, Tara Fee, Rebecca Morgan Frank, Rebecca Hazelton, L. S. Klatt, Christopher Kondrich, Adam Latham, Cate Lycurgus, Matt Morton, Sarah Rose Nordgren, John Poch, Wyatt Prunty, Joshua Robbins, Bobby C. Rogers, Michael Shewmaker, James Smith, Lisa Russ Spaar, Caki Wilkinson, Ryan Wilson, Kathleen Winter, and David Yezzi.

Thanks also to the institutions that have supported my writing during the years in which these poems were composed, especially the Sewanee Writers' Conference, Valparaiso University, and Washington & Jefferson College.

Greatest thanks to my wife, my family, and to my God.

NEWLY

NOT

ETERNAL

Mosquito

God was only acting godly
when he strapped a dirty needle
to the fly
and taught it how to curtsy
on our knees and elbows

on our necks and earlobes
so politely that it hardly
stirs an eye.
God was hard but speaking softly
when He told us we should die.

A Few Keys

This is the key
to my pickup
and this is the key
to my home.
The key to my laptop
is letters and symbols;
my birthdate's the key
to my phone.
I once stole a key
to a diary
and once turned a key
made of bone.
What this key can do
I've forgotten.
This key is some other
key's clone.

This key takes the form
of a feather;
it swings the green doors
in the roofs of these oaks.
This match is the key
to an altar
and frees a black
serpent of smoke.
This key is the bronze
in my brown left eye,
but what's shuttered
tonight is unclear.
This key is the pitch
and the torque
of my voice. May it fit
in a favorable ear.

If these coins make a key
to the turnpike,
the tollbooth's
a bribable latch.
So, a vein is impressed
by a needle,
and hardwood
submits to an axe.
But you can't coax a mind
with an order
or force belief
loose with a fact.
When I've turned, it's the teeth
in a bittersweet song,
their diligent
baffle and scratch.

This last key of course
is a wristwatch.
I turn it by sitting
stock still,
by letting the clouds
turn around me,
by adding more drinks
to my bill.
Eventually everything
opens: the blue
fist of evening, the maw
in these rocks.
With a click
it all fastens
behind me. This last key
is also a lock.

Song of the Imaginary Friend

Give me
your gall. Give me
an ugly name,

the fabric
body of a tragic
doll,

yarn-haired,
bug-eyed, plain.
I'll take the blame.

I'll think the thoughts
you shouldn't
claim, the bald

abuse and aimless
libel—
I'm the cloth

and Lysol
used to disinfect
a brain.

Give me
your stains and sweat,
your small wet cough

against my neck,
your spit,
your kiss's mange.

I'll nip back soft:
my lips
a waft of light

against your jaw
while you're asleep.
I'll bare

my teeth,
but barely. Where
a parasite

might gnaw,
might thieve, I only
want my share

of why
you're lonely, Mother,
God. My bite

is fair. Give me
the grief
to which I'm heir.

Shiversong

Given snow
that doesn't flinch
to throw its pounds
through heaven inch
by inch, that sows
a billion motes
of chill into
this ground man can't
defend; and given
wind that won't
begin to tell
us how it's driven,
where it fell from,
what it's meant
to blow and which
proud limbs the clouds
want riven since
it doesn't dimly
know, or even
why the howling
whims have pardoned
us thus far;
given such,
it's hard to watch
the black-eyed scarecrow
some fool left here
miming care
above the blighted
garden, though
tonight he seems
intent to wrack
the soil and climb
the air, to fly,

to crash his flimsy
cross against
the deadpan rancor
in the vast
grim sky.

Migraine

　　　　Unless the temples tremble,
this brain burns

few prayers, and this mind
　　　　minds no shiny Bible

　　　　when the kind God's there.
It's hurt that earns

attention. This hot
　　　　vein behind this eyeball

　　　　only learns alertness
by its pain,

and there's a tender
　　　　tinder near this ear

　　　　whose nothing-nature's
never won a name,

though now its livid suffering
　　　　proves it's dear.

　　　　The hour's dear
in which this brow's an altar,

sweating gall
　　　　like gasoline to grease

the humbled mass of me
in flames I'll falter

out of when the graceful
burner's eased.

An aimless grief then?
This head wouldn't say so:

the blazing briefly
wreathes me in its halo.

Still Life

Peculiar how the olio
of days and rain and sun
inside a grape can taste
so much like time itself,
a liberal age distilled
to what one swallow
will erase; strange
in apples that same mix
seems mostly crisp,
clear water in its wildest
form, while peaches
clench their sugar
in a ghostly wattage,
fossil brightness
slightly warm.

Summer's ending
and again I'm older.
For several minutes
it's been faintly raining,
though the blunt,
blithe sunlight's
undiminished.
Something weather-baked
inside me smolders
toward forever:
one wet grape remaining
in the bowl
when this quick
picnic's finished.

Little Black Bouquet

1. DIM TIME

The small of her back when the lights were dim
was an idle clock. For losing time

my sentence now is a thousand hymns
to the small of her. The lights go dim

and hours slip from the dial's rim.
I've wound my life till remorse is primed

in the small of my back. When the lights are dim,
an idle clock still loosens time.

2. MUSE

She whispers thistles in his ear,
and when she leaves, her whistling blisters.

She's elsewhere till he volunteers
his eyes and tongue to bear her thistles.

Though she quotes new lovers, calls him *dear,*
by dawn his wounds already miss her.

Her thistles whisper in his ear
and when he breathes his blisters whistle.

3. ISCARIOT'S PSALM

The only way one kills a God
is by obtaining his permission.

Submit that he will rise. Applaud
his lonely way. To kill a god
you coax him from the flesh façade.

I saw the veil torn in a vision
of the only way my kiss kills God:

with him ordaining my perdition.

Song of the Guardian Angel

I've tried to pace
the hurry
in your breast

as thirty thousand
reps a day
I weigh

your breath.
I gray your hair,
assign you debts,

and hold the blade
that pares
your prime away

in sighs, dead skin,
and sweat.
Like a silent clock

I'm always talking,
duly tic
the same

two saws: *pause now,*
and *pray.*
Until you stop

inside forever, I
prescribe
you shame.

I don't dislike you,
but you'll not
be missed.

Less wasteful charges
are the child
who ends

at birth,
the bed-sore
comatose with mist

for brains
who master haste.
They comprehend

my patience,
they restate,
in sum, my case,

but you,
so rushed through time,
stay numb to grace.

The First Supper

Newly not eternal,
        newly partly
past, he's here by way
        of forty weeks
inside another volatile
        physique.
He's purple, then he quickly
        pinks and hardly
breathes before we see
        he's breathing fine.
It's only seconds
        till he's at her breast—
the sweet colostrum
        like a spurt of fresh
infinity injected
        into time.

While his mother's left hand
        cups his puckered feet,
her right palm guides him
        to this cup his birth
has made her. It's an image
        she rehearsed
all night as each worse spasm
        struck its peak,
as blood spilled, body broke,
        and she defeated
labor so her urgent son
        could nurse.

Noon

A tall, dry
    waterfall of gleam
        pretends
it's clearly righteous
    light and not
        at all
the lie it is.

    When thought heaps
        up in wind
and thunder,
    my relief
        is thinking small
enough to
    sleep it off
        in cotton sheets.
When thought might ice,
    I thaw
        with alcohol
and cheat
    the thermostat
        a few degrees.
If thinking fogs,
    I take a later
        flight.

I want
    more wisdom less
        than I want ease.

But then the candid
      noon is only
           right
when I don't stare.
      If my regard
           ascends
that clarity
      and sheer
           high Fahrenheit,
I see
      its blinding logic's
           mindless end.

I ought to doubt
      the truth
           I comprehend.

Hot Minute

So bright now
on this shadeless
cul-de-sac
of time,
my near-bald neighbor
at his mailbox
wipes his brow
and sighs
as light's unveiled
vendetta
scalds our ill-used
fescue black.
There's not
one clement letter
in these stacks
of bills and ads
for short-term,
red-hot sales,
and not a wisp
of rescue
through the stale
white sky
which only retails
sweat and lack.

A breath ago
the whole hale street
was greened
from curb
to bungalow,

a glazy-sheened
Arcadia,
a burb
where even cynics
beamed
and elsewhere's highs
were quarantined
in haze. . . .

Now only feels
so hot a minute
when it's clear
we braise
forever in it.

Ambitious Circumcision

Carve a soft ring of skin off
my penis.
Nip a lobe of pink meat off
my spleen.
Lop the tip of my peacocking
tongue off.
Pare the sex and the race off
my genes.

Put the scalpel to each of
my fingers
and peel back their singular
whorls.
Cut the consciousness clean from
my ego.
Flense my last layer of self off
the world.

If they're true, make my meager
thoughts holy
by letting the name on them
fade.
Work the sharp second hand of
a wall clock
to shave me off
whatever I've made.

Song of the Genie

I lake the drought.
  I bake flood off again.
I make fools rich enough
  that for a while
they fool the rich enough
  to dictate style.
I beautify. I muscle up.
  I thin.
I pheromone.
  I woo. I violin
the mood. I penthouse suite
  and private isle.
I ease death out of view,
  but never smile,
and only everlast
  what's always been.

The books and movies
  are confused, of course.
It's my warm, timeworn rag
  that rubs your mind
to force the rank wish free:
  voracious, blind,
and magnetized
  to bankruptcy, divorce,
exhaust fumes primed
  into the past-due Porsche.
At last I'd grant you you,
  but you decline.

Black Igloo

The shadows thrown
by snowcaps here are thin

as hose, as onionskin,
and what the clouds

cast massive over town
is not so proud

that it won't scatter
once the South howls in.

At two the street-lit lawn
still squints our shades;

by dawn the focal
watts of sunshot want

to soak us in their flashy
spill, to flaunt

light's violence past
the glass and chintz blockades.

For rest, we'll need
an umbra old enough

to stand, a feat of cold
in loam-dark bricks

paroled from antique
drawers and frosted fixed

with all the chrome
eclipses we can slough

off sleep by hand. We'll leave
no doors, no cracks.

We'll steep our eyes
beneath a dome of black.

Ultrasound: Your Picture

Henry Thomas Clark, 10/7/14

We've framed an ultrasound
     of you and Peter

holding hands
     (or almost) in the womb,

your moon-bright arms
     crossed in a black balloon

with week, and weights,
     and heights in millimeters

penciled on the side.
     We say it's good

that he, at least, was with you
     when you died,

that unlike us
     you'll never know the why

of being lonely
     or what naked falsehood

feels like in one's mind.
     You see, it's false

to say your death
     was somehow grace. It's grace

that spared Cain's life
       and later gave Eve other

sons, despite creation's
       wastes and faults.

I wish you could have known
       love's aftertastes.

I wish you'd had a chance
       to hate your brother.

Virga

God's vault's been dry
so long some angels doubt

rain ever coming back.
Now their own songs

must slake them: one hymn
explains what they did wrong,

but not convincingly;
another pouts

in country twang
with metaphors about

the dearth of decent
cloudscapes since He's gone;

their favorites, though,
boast instrumental yawns

and high vibratos
that defy the drought.

It isn't much
as worship goes. They frown

despite their lifted hands
and unfurled wings.

Still, better that than keen
like mortal things:

just now one shameless seraph
weeps dawn down

and shines a stretch of air
in wispy strings—

a fine, bright prayer
that never hits the ground.

Ultrasound: Your Mirror

I wish you'd had a chance
     to hate your brother's

charming smile.
     Sometimes his laugh would chafe

against your own; his tears
     would misbehave

across your cheeks; his lisp
     might cue your stutter.

Nights, in the mirror
     you'd have seen your lovers

kiss his lips, and mornings,
     as you'd shave,

you'd nick yourself
     and wonder who forgave

you when the face you shared
     caused him to suffer.

No. No childhood scars
     will make it clearer

which you are.
     We have the future tense

for Peter, while you're left
     at one night less

than one night old,
        my son without a likeness,

who I can't hold
        or half-behold, condensed

to shadows in the nursery's
        lightless mirror.

Ultrasound: Your Shadows

The shadows in the nursery's
          lifeless mirror

owe their gray to no one;
          you were gone

before the lights
          could pin those umbras on.

If now they gather here
          in tangles sheerer

than a nest of nylon
          hose, yet nearer

flesh than atmosphere,
          they must be drawn

as I am by the dimmed
          lamp's denouement—

this stupid wish your guise
          might still cohere or

that some phantom wisp
          would throw its shade

and let the smallest
          sliver of you loom

against the wall. Instead,
          the day exhumes

this catch of bruises
        till they've all been weighed

and matched to furniture.
        My shape has stayed

to spill your name
        into the empty room.

Small God

Small enough to crawl
in through the pet door

to my mind when I'm
all locked, so small

it nests a migraine
in my pillow, galls

my hallways like a noisy
clock, or, better,

it's a doll and I'm the child
who would forget her

in a closet
though she coo and call

left *on*, her voice box
yawing till the drawl

dissolves to empty howl,
a silent letter.

Except tonight the volume's
swelled, grown stronger,

prouder, as the house
around it hushed—

alarms always seem loudest
when they're wrong.

I damn the wrecked detector
wailing on,

but then there's smoke.
Constricting rooms combust,

and God's too big
to hide here any longer.

Ultrasound: Your Room

I spill your name
      into the empty room

and make the place more
      empty still: the chair's

clean seat adopts
      a misanthropic air

that mocks the bureau's
      sympathetic bloom.

I watch the wooden crib
      as it's consumed

by morning, bar by bar,
      till crying downstairs

lets me know
      how far this solitary

staring has erased
      me in the gloom.

Your healthy twin
      is hungry, tired, parched

and wet, or simply
      needing to be held,

and yet I still don't move.
      I feel compelled

to tell the room
     it's missing you, to mark

the vacuum with a few
     more decibels

of Henry, Henry,
     Henry Thomas Clark.

God Jokes

God's jokes are lost
on us. Although He laughs,

is even halfway silly
sometimes—case

in point: giraffes—
His humor lacks a face.

There's little human
in the aftermath,

and no wry pout: "just kidding."
No dumb gaffes

we might relate to,
no punch lines, and no trace

of any doubt.
He doesn't self-efface.

His gags (who's laughing
now?) are often wraths:

incensed volcanoes,
cities rinsed in baths

of fire and ash;
or voids, the stains in space,

a grave inside a womb.
And though his grace

(we must believe)
is worked on our behalf,

it pains us too.
We weep at His embrace

and strain to hear
Him crying while He laughs.

Ultrasound: Your Names

My Henry, Henry,
      Henry Thomas Clark:

your name's an ingot—
      if I even think it

after midnight
      in the bedroom's dark,

the graceless kiln my mind is
      fires to sing it

out of shape, to turn
      its sounds to trinkets

or just smelt it down
      to question marks

so I can ladle up
      that pink and drink it

till my ears drown
      and the dreaming starts.

Your sister's "Gemma-
      Lemon" in her fruit

pajamas, Georgie-Boy's
      my little buddy,

and Pete these days
      is simply "The Recruit."

Beneath my desk
      you'd be my understudy,

"Huffy Hank" in tears,
      or "Huckleputty"

sweetly teething
      on your mom's Bluetooth.

Ultrasound: Your Urn

Tonight Pete's teething
      on your mom's Bluetooth.

He found the scissors
      to derange his hair.

We've left the gate
      down and he's on the stairs,

or else he's scrambled
      up a dollhouse roof.

The crumpled books
      and cracker crumbs are proof

he's loose . . . disordered
      blocks, a toppled chair. . . .

Some days he's absolutely
      everywhere

until I wish him gone,
      to tell the truth.

Not you. You stay
      exactly as you're left:

the tame and quiet twin,
      the easy one,

the boy who never
      makes a mess, the son

whose whispered name
  will be our shibboleth

for innocence, whose
  only fault is done,

who never cries, or fights,
  or takes a breath.

Loud Outs

No one lofts a loud out
    to the left field

fencing with its ads
    for Meacham's Auto

and McClintock Paints.
    There's no bravado

at the plate at all.
    No southpaw deals

his slider for a strike
    no one appeals,

since no one lent
    the anthem her vibrato.

This afternoon the high,
    off-tune legato

in the stands is only
    wind on steel.

But even though the team's
    gone out of town

and mind forever,
    though a storm is spinning

this way now, and though
    the world's beginning

to dissolve in dust purled
    off the mound,

a patience rallies
    and the dark spills down

another hour
    and an extra inning.

Ultrasound: Your Image

You never cry, or fight,
      or take a breath,

but you wreck pictures
      just like any child.

These days our crowded
      foregrounds show the cleft

and no amount
      of staging reconciles

the family's best
      lopsided photo ops.

Your mom, positioning
      one shot, remarks,

Just think how this would look
      with Henry propped

in Daddy's lap—
      this picture needs six Clarks.

Of course, we have
      the images we took

in the recovery room
      when nurses brought

your body in your blanket,
      but I won't look

at those. You're in these others,
　　though you're not:

our half-filled stroller
　　is a double-seater.

We framed the ultrasound
　　of you and Peter.

The Statue Gardens

The year we're thirty-three
a sculpture in our likeness
is installed within the gardens.
Hard to say exactly
what it honors. High bluffs
block prevailing winds
along the lakeshore here,
and mornings, drowned in fog,
the scattered statuary
on the lawns resembles nothing
quite so much as loneliness
solidified: cloud-bound,
even showgirls loom
like gargoyles. Iron lamps line
the paths and throw peculiar
shadows on the grass
at night. Spooked, we seem
unsure how to respond.
As posted, it's illegal
to deface a civil statue,
but there's often lewd
graffiti on the priests.
Last fall, a fractured soldier
flaunted law to sledge
his double's arms to rubble—
no one stopped or shamed him.
Once, a mother, livid,
wrecked her husband's coupe
against the womanizer's
pedestal, then wept
over his shattered feet
until authorities
arrived to take her home.

It's spring again, or nearly,
when our young men play
at patricide, targeting
their fathers' alabaster
hearts with family rifles.
The night's one-sided gunfire,
like a corporate hiccup,
jogs the restive burg.

But blessings too accrue here.
Of late, a blind girl comes
at dawn to hold our hardened
features in her hands.
For several clement weeks
the heartthrob by the lilacs
wore a dozen shades
of lipstick on his neck
(his shoulder, earlobes, hip)
until a rain reset
his decency. Beneath
a pair of lacebark elms,
a green-gray woman throws
her head back, infinitely
laughing. Hummingbirds
bathe in the hollow there
behind her teeth and preen
until the rock appears
to sing beyond our hearing.
The street musician busks
outside the hippodrome
till dark, but when the crowd
disperses, he reports
to the line of pink azaleas

where a marble violin case
tenders the gratuity
his statue's earned in silence.

Gerberas pop this last
week in July. Fog
cooks off by nine, and summer
chokes the garden paths
with tourists in their shorts.
By noon the statues flag.
Exhausted and resigned,
their mien is more like bleary
zoo life than like art—
the wide world narrowed
to a solitary ego,
each two-foot plinth a cage.
And more exhibits added
Sunday every week.

From across the central green
I watch the ceremonies
that reveal our fresh
immortals. Once the mayor
has said his bit and duly
prayed, a drape's whipped off.
Yesterday, on stage,
one guest of honor balked
as sometimes (often) happens.
Clearly this was not
the image he had hoped for,
though all his friends and family
praised the likeness. Posed
in suit and tie, the figure

cleans its turbid glasses
with a handkerchief.
A softness to the smile
and the angle of the head
suggest it might be tuned
to music or a voice
that it enjoys. And yet
there's something in the shoulders,
in the posture, not at ease.
Something it would say,
and feel better saying,
if an intimate could listen.

It's commonplace to swear
the sculptures see what mirrors
can't, but I suspect
we each believe our case
is an exception, at least
to some degree. The artists
interview our friends
and, if the rumor's true,
surveil us too. How else
explain the apprehension
on display in our First Lady's
peerless smile? When she's
in motion it's invisible,
but her statue only almost
hides a kind of inner
wrinkle just beneath
the surface of the marble.
The subtlety's impressive,
and we rightly praise
the craftsmanship, but lately

I have wondered if
a nuanced disaffection's
simply native to the stone.
Either none of us
are restful, or contentment
foils the finest chisels.
Even those arrested
in the midst of pleasure
have an air of vague
distress when one stands close.
We like to point this out,
then move a little closer.

Most regulars will visit
later in the evenings,
but I like to catch
the gardens still asleep.
It was cool this morning,
breezeless, visibility
as low as thirty feet.
And though the park lights hazed
away to halos, yellow
tree frogs sounded out
the lawns from every wrist
and collarbone. The lake
is high this year, and more
than once the cloudy surf
unrolled over my boots.
Figures I had never
seen before appeared
among the reeds: a sailor,
fishermen, a bather
whose wet hair extended

past her waist. The water
lapped unhurriedly
against eroded ankles,
and in the blurry coolness
off the lake, the statues dripped.

When we pass, our families
are encouraged to collect
our likeness for display
at home, but not all do,
and some of the deceased
remain among the living.
Other effigies
retire to less august
locations. In the brothel
one pays something extra
for the room that stocks a nun.
And in the jail downtown,
a famous convict leans
forever in a corner
of the holding cell:
they say a hundred years
ago the man broke out
three times, but he was always
caught again, and now
the grooves scored in his chest
read, "Model Prisoner."

My own rock's one of several
near the bluffs, and yet
sometimes my vision's fooled
to think he's rearranged
his stance and moved. I'll see

a figure with that light
patina on its shoulders,
or some half-congruent
silhouette, and always,
as I look again, the same
sensation: that he's not me
at all and merely trying
to escape this place he's bound
in by mistake. You hear
two maxims commonly:
that with each year we grow
to be more like them, and
that every year the stones
grow more estranged. Clichés
that miss the point and can't
explain the simultaneous
self-love and animosity
that keeps most citizens
away while others come
here daily. I left the shore
this morning and retreated
past the vetch and roses
on my way to work.
There I saw the blind girl,
older than I'd thought
and rapt in concentration,
peeling, flake by flake,
a purple lichen off
her lovely statue's face.

Black Light

Let's call this your exotic shine debut:
       your lipstick neon
and your teeth ice blue,
a dress designed to slice
       through déjà vu,
your shoulder's pink-lined scorpion tattoo.

You came to sip a teal cocktail or two.
       You came to plumb
what might be real in lieu
of all that is too slightly.
       You're trying to
distinguish finally how to be, or who.

This isn't vision's clumsy pas de deux
       with sight, that long, gray
wrong-way rendezvous.
UV upends the eye
       in your IQ
till seeing clears. A dark sea swells through you.

Black skews the vantage of more candid views.
       White's lies you know;
this light makes knowledge new.

The Latch

We nurse our secrets
and their suckle hurts.

Since birth the two top teeth
are white and keen

as science in fluorescent
lights. Our shirts

are wrenched; the shamed
breasts tend mastitic, mean

all night and febrile
when those pink lips purse

at two a.m.
to drop the guillotine

of appetite. Of course
what's most perverse

is that it would burn more
to tell, to wean

the creatures off
our silence—milky blue

and warm, a carnal
dribble at their chins.

Each leaks a cry
so innocent and thin

that only we, attached,
can taste the *ooh*.

Behind the latch, as sharp
and sweet as sin,

the hard mouth needs us,
and it feeds us too.

Washing Your Feet

Stranger, they are dirty.
    You've come so far
so harshly: bloody miles
    through silt and brambles,
noxious bogs and mud-fields,
    dunes of char
beneath the sun-spill—
    all of it in sandals.

Please take my chair;
    this dry blond Scotch on ice
will douse your pride.
    I kneel to yawn the straps
that bite your ankles,
    loose the vamps that vise
your tarsals, slide
    bruised heels into my lap.

There's fragrant water
    in the wooden vessel,
sanded smooth and gauged
    so that your stride
can lose its travel
    in the lather's pestle
and cascade. You're no one,
    and you're special,
drawn to leave
    before you're even dried,
the paths bathed off
    revealing paths inside.

Original Sins

Does everyone choose lesser imitations
of their loves over the originals since
Eden? I'd wish my bride into a woman
I despise and eat my share of original sin.

♣

The trick of licorice is how it kinks
its sugar with a snakebite. The trick of gin
is that it wraps your mind in mink.
Mixed, the barkeep calls them an "original sin."

♣

In the film, the man is good who clones himself.
It's his clone that's twisted (scissors in its grin).
The knotted denouement finds one man dead,
one weeping: the clone merely the original's sins.

♣

Our apiarists now can gentle swarms
of Africanized bees by introducing docile, virgin
queens into aggressive hives, if first they cull
the former sovereigns, the original sins.

♣

We were the exact same band, same songs,
but we found more and better fans
once Adam got arrested for possession
and we changed our name to The Original Sins.

♣

They're rarer than the glass-winged butterflies
that ghost through Panama like bobby pins,
but in the holy drowse of his confessional,
a listless priest is dreaming of original sins.

Impeccable musicians are not psalmists,
though their fluencies are God's. Men's
voices haunt the angels when, like David's,
they are ravaged by a passion, in all praise
                    or in all sin.

Eyelash

Awfully late and we were naked
when I plucked it off your cheekbone,

bee-leg thin and hard to see
and oddly heated on my thumb.

Scratched across your grainy shadow,
it ignited like a match.

You drew close and pinched the flame out.
Petals bloomed against my hand,

a yellow rose, but not for long
without a vase to frame its pomp.

Held so near our gin martinis,
it became a twist of lemon;

by the time we finished drinking,
just a crumpled cigarette.

Blue to pale, the bedroom curtains;
you and I were different too.

A new economy of romance
balmed our worries in the gloom.

Against a warm vein it turned needle,
tiny serpent at your breast,

then pen to plume to paring knife:
a kind of talisman roulette.

I held the blade up to the window
and its beveled edge went white.

Enough, you sighed, and puffed away
that slightest sliver of this life.

Gardensong

in the gardens
     in the gardens
you are walking
     you are walking
through the roses
     to the roses

you are almost
     you are talking
in a whisper
     like a whisper
to the roses
     through the roses

now you're leaving
     and you're leaving
through the tulips
     through the tulips
night is falling
     lightly falling

bye to you
     goodbye to you
by the pansies
     'side the pansies
by the pansies
     bye to you

Elsewhen

Their roads will waste to grass
　　　because—no cars.

They'll rarely taste raw air,
　　　or not at all,

connecting through a gleaming
　　　blue-glass wall

that manifests their flawless
　　　avatars.

Their bodies too will suffer
　　　fewer scars,

preserved from outside germs,
　　　from sun and falls,

by smart-foam clothes and safety
　　　protocols.

They'll much prefer it
　　　to the way we are.

Just as we would rather
　　　happen now

than back when families shared
　　　a one-room house,

when they were old at forty,
　　　wrinkled, gray,

and there was only starlight
    in the clouds.

Aware, of course, there would be
    other ways,

they dreamed about
    and dreaded us today.

Kaleidoscope

Light, break my eye
already fractured by

desire, already
splintered into squints

and silvers as it's
raked along a thigh,

already only slivers
of the wince

inside my smile. Light,
spit in dust, apply

the mud into my sight,
and cake me blind

enough to witness
all a pupil hides.

Light, shake the iris
out my eye; remind

me it's a guise.
And as a swatter pins

a fly's against the window—
every lens

brought flat before
a broad white sky, amended

from distraction
to a final splendid

sigh—Light, ache
my eye past all pretense

until its lies rinse
out and I transcend it.

Sun on Your Shoulders

May
      this
reck-
      less
sum
      of
sum-
      mer
freck-
      les
kiss
      by
kiss
      be-
come
      a
neck-
      lace.

Poltergeists

They move my keys
where I can't find them.
Their expertise
is reassigning

items where
they shouldn't be:
the lost stuffed bear
in a chemise

under a load
of laundry, phone
in the commode.
When I'm alone

(it's rare these days)
I feel their tiny
shadows play
across my mind

and then my thoughts
are disarranged.
The logic-knots
I'd tied have changed

into a mess
of crayon swirls
that paint, I guess,
a little girl

beside her dad.
The ghosts are cruel,
but I'm not mad,
not quite. They're fools

and hard to see though,
not yet half-solid
in their egos.
Tonight, the squalid

den is evidence
that they've been busy:
one's dispensed
the box of Disney

heroines
across my chair.
The genuine
girl-ghost is there

herself, and stands
against the wall.
She hides her hand
and one last doll

behind the sheer
white drapes. She wants
to disappear.
Her father haunts

this room. He'll chide
her and then fade
his head inside
the books displayed

on shelves out of her
reach. Or perhaps
he'll call her brother,
move both ghouls

out of place:
into his lap
until the rules
have been erased.

Postcard from Home

The birds in our county were bees
and the bees were rough nuggets of light.
The green ponds we soaked in were trees
and the thunderheads' bellies were white.

The sky was a bowl of pink grapefruit.
Your house was all threshold and eaves.
When a distance consumed and erased you,
the kudzu here sputtered and seethed.

Remember June's scorchy pervasions?
That chill only sweat can achieve?
The fires at our feet were impatiens.
Through the legs of our shorts ran a breeze.

Wherever your luster has blown to,
wherever your ebbing proceeds,
there's our hollow that's filled you and known you,
this nowhere that saunters and preens.

In the sunflower's eye stands a hornet.
In the stray's empty socket, a flea.
In a brilliance where vision is forfeit,
my eye lays its hand on your knee.

Afterhere

Zealot's yawn?
Xeroxed worship?

Vapid, utterly
tamed Sabbaths?

Religion's quaintly
painted otherworld?

No.

More likely,
kismet's jackpot

isn't hackneyed
gibberish for

eternity. Death's
clichés belabor

alleluias.

Midnight

So the road dead-
        ends into
this northern vista.

You can't go
        further than
the panorama's

edge:
        its virgin snow,
that ice-jam twisted

through the firs
        below whose matching
fleece pajamas

gently let you
        know you're far
too pledged

to all the heat
        at home,
the days you owe

and lease
        and nearly own.
Atop this ledge

the wind is stiff,
        and then it starts
to blow.

But even if
        before
you've stopped right here

and winced as each
        tomorrow
déjà vued,

tonight you sense
        a yawn
in the frontier,

which tempts you to
        the fence
and slides you through.

Glance back and watch
        your boot prints
disappear:

the long
        hand inches on,
but not on you.

Yestermorrow

Hallelujah, it's nobody's birthday!
Nobody's wedding and nobody's wake!
For once the glib calendar's dumb.
These brave hours have sloughed off their date.

No unions are striking, no voters are polled,
Though if anything dawn has come early.
While the coffee is yet to be ground,
our displeasures dissolve prematurely.

We're a people with bleachers to get to,
outlets to enter, entrées to eat,
but this morning it's clear to anyone:
nothing's planned and there's nowhere to be.

If the wind at the backs of our minds is persuasive,
still each destination feels wrong.
We wander outside in our boxers
to stand at the edge of our lawns.

Hallelujah, that here on mortality's turf
the daily's been soundly defeated!
The diaries are shredded inside us.
The dockets have balked and retreated.

Any vows we have made to each other
melt away in our mouths like confections
and at once they're replaced by the knowledge
that at last we're immune to deception.

The day picks up its skirts with its eyes closed,
eventful, though nothing will count.
I hear fireworks rebound one street over.
The DeWhitts, in their front yard, make out.

As local balloonists are coasting their baskets
to rest in the neighborhood park,
our children eject from the tire swings
and gently tear heaven apart.

Even when dusk sizzles through the azaleas
the day feels unwilling to end.
Stars flicker back out in the cypress.
The moon seems inclined to descend.

Hallelujah, the networks have cancelled the news
with no scandals, invasions, or earthquakes!
What's next we'll discover in time,
when eternity turns into Thursday.